ANN MORRIS

◆◆◆◆◆◆◆◆◆◆◆◆◆◆◆◆◆◆◆◆◆◆

TEAMWORK

LOTHROP, LEE & SHEPARD BOOKS

NEW YORK

Special thanks to Lawrence G. Myers for his inspiration and advice

The author wishes to thank the following for the use of their photographs: front jacket—Comstock Inc./David Lokey; Woodfin Camp & Associates and their photographers: pp. 1, 14—Timothy Eagan, p. 2—Paul Solomon, pp. 6, 9, 24, 25—John Eastcott/Yva Momatiuk, p. 7 (left)—Mike Yamashita, p. 8—Martin Rogers, pp. 10 (left), 17 (right), 19, 23 (left), 27 (inset)—Ken Heyman, p. 13—A. Ramey, p. 15 (bottom)—Thomas L. Kelly, p. 18 (left)—Susan Lapides; p. 5—Heidi Larson; p. 7 (right)—© Oliver Benn/Tony Stone Images; p. 10 (right)—© Oldrich Karasek/Tony Stone Images; p. 11—© Alain Le Garsmeur/Tony Stone Images; pp. 12, 20 (left)—SuperStock, Inc.; p. 15 (top)—Animals Animals © Norbert Rosing; pp. 16, 17 (left)—AP/Wide World Photos; p. 18 (top right)—© Will & Deni McIntyre/Tony Stone Images; p. 21—© Joseph McBride/Tony Stone Images; p. 22—© Bruce Ayres/Tony Stone Images; p. 23 (right)—David Archer; p. 26—© Nicholas DeVore/Tony Stone Images; p. 27 (right)—© Penny Tweedie/Tony Stone Images; p. 28—United Nations Photo 180751/M. Grant; back jacket—© James Strachan/Tony Stone Images.

Text copyright © 1999 by Ann Morris

Published by Lothrop, Lee & Shepard Books
a division of William Morrow and Company, Inc.
1350 Avenue of the Americas, New York, NY 10019
www.williammorrow.com

Printed in Hong Kong by South China Printing Company (1988) Ltd.

10 9 8 7 6 5 4 3 2 1

Library of Congress Cataloging-in-Publication Data
Morris, Ann.
Teamwork/Ann Morris.
p. cm.
Summary: Discusses teamwork and how team members working
together as a group cooperate to get the job done.
ISBN 0-688-16551-6 (trade)—ISBN 0-688-16995-3 (library)
1. Teams in the workplace—Juvenile literature. 2. Social groups—Juvenile literature.
[1. Teams in the workplace.] I. Title.
HD66.M67 1999 302.3'4—dc21 98-46996 CIP AC

TEAMWORK

A team is a group that works together . . .

or plays together.

Team members cooperate to get the job done.
That's called **teamwork.**

A team can be just a few . . .

or a team can be many.

Even animals can work in teams.

Some teams wear uniforms.

Others do not.

Teams plan together
to make things
come out right.

Team members depend on one another.

Team members are proud of one another.

Each team member is part of a whole.

Teamwork makes the job easier.

Teamwork gets the job done.

The best team of all is the family—

working together,
playing together,
caring for one
another.

And the biggest and most important team
is the **world's** family—
all the world's nations working together
to help one another,
to solve problems,
to make peace.

INDEX

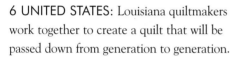

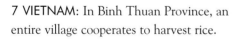

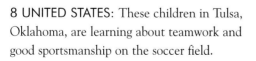

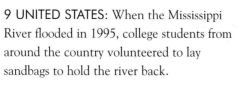

17 UNITED STATES: Chicago Bulls' Michael Jordan, top, passes to a teammate as the Bulls and Utah Jazz square off in game one of the NBA Finals, in Salt Lake City on June 3, 1998.

17 UNITED STATES: It's never hard to pull together a basketball team in New York City.

18 UNITED STATES: At this farm and wilderness camp, campers plan together to make sure that what they're building comes out right.

19 UNITED STATES: This gospel choir in Winston-Salem, North Carolina, practices for many hours to make their performances perfect.

19 JAPAN: This Japanese film company is producing a comedy. The actors' moves and the camera angles are planned in advance.

20 UNITED STATES: Mountain-climbing teams, like this one climbing near Eagle Lake in California, depend on one another for their lives.

21 UNITED STATES: Sky divers thousands of feet in the air above patchwork fields in Davis, California, demonstrate a stylistic link-together called *relative work*.

22 UNITED STATES: Team members celebrate a home run.

23 INDONESIA: This group of girls in a dance school in Ubud, on the island of Bali, rehearses for an upcoming festival.

23 UNITED STATES: New York's West Side Otters learn about teamwork in the Little League at Riverside Park.

24 CANADA: Cod fishermen in Newfoundland work together in the cold waters of the North Atlantic.

25 CZECHOSLOVAKIA: A team of people works with a team of horses at haying time.

26 INDONESIA: All aboard and hold on tight! This daddy in Bali is taking the whole family for a ride!

27 PUERTO RICO: The entire family sits down to enjoy *Abuelita*'s (Grandmother's) cooking—and each other.

27 MALAWI: This little boy in Tengani Camp helps his mother pound grain.

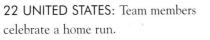

28 UNITED STATES: The United Nations General Assembly meets in New York City. They work to maintain peace and friendly cooperation among the nations of the world.

Where in the world were these photographs taken?

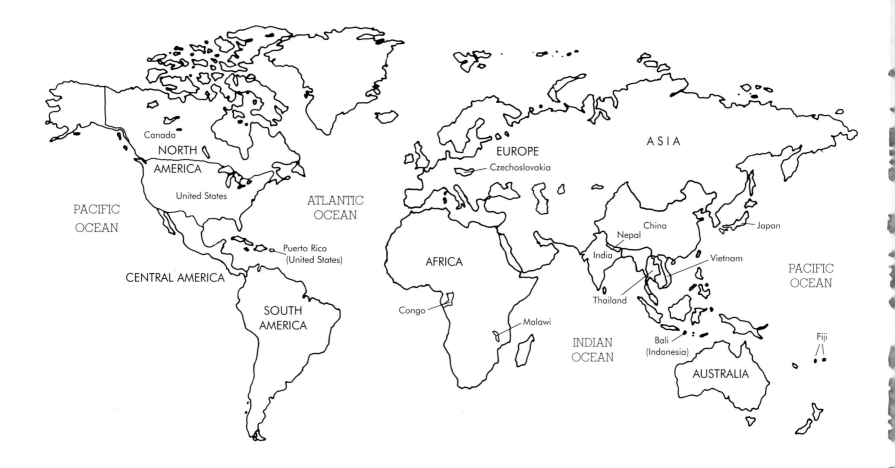

Canada

NORTH
AMERICA

United States

PACIFIC
OCEAN

CENTRAL AMERICA

SOUTH
AMERICA

ATLANTIC
OCEAN

Puerto Rico
(United States)

AFRICA

Congo

Malawi

EUROPE

Czechoslovakia

ASIA

China

Nepal

Japan

India

Vietnam

Thailand

INDIAN
OCEAN

Bali
(Indonesia)

AUSTRALIA

PACIFIC
OCEAN

Fiji